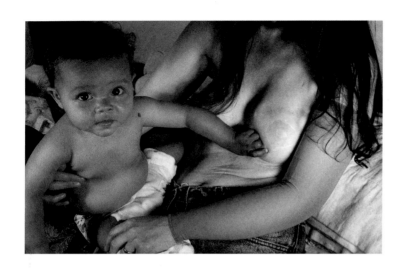
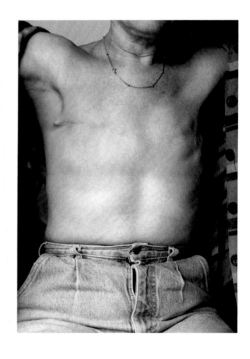

AMELIA DAVIS

the first look

Foreword by Nancy Snyderman, M.D.
Contributions by Loren Eskenazi, M.D., F.A.C.S.
and Saskia R. J. Thiadens, R.N.

UNIVERSITY OF ILLINOIS PRESS   URBANA AND CHICAGO

Publication of this book was generously supported by a
grant from the William E. Weiss Foundation, Inc.

Library of Congress Cataloging-in-Publication Data
Davis, Amelia, 1968–
The first look / Amelia Davis ; foreword by Nancy
Snyderman ; contributions by Loren Eskenazi and
Saskia R. J. Thiadens.
    p.   cm.
Includes bibliographical references.
ISBN 0-252-02602-0 (cloth : acid-free paper) —
ISBN 0-252-06925-0 (paper : acid-free paper)
1. Breast—Cancer—Patients—Portraits. I. Title.
RC280.B8D3628   2000
362.1'9699449'00222—dc21   00-008763

1 2 3 4 5 C P 5 4 3 2 1

for my mother

You are missed, but never forgotten.

You are my hero.

contents

foreword

Nancy Snyderman, M.D.

When I was a little girl I always wondered why artists, when painting or sculpting, would concentrate on the female breast, often to the exclusion of other parts of the female anatomy. I noticed how little attention was paid to the sexual organs of men. As a teenager I was outraged and saw the disparity as sexist. Were women sculpted and painted with bare breasts because the majority of artists were men? Maybe. But perhaps my interpretation was painted with too broad a brush stroke.

As I grew out of my adolescent body and into the one I have occupied as a woman, my views changed. I have come to believe that the female breast has been depicted in many shapes and sizes and with such adoration because it is beautiful and represents so much to us as a culture and to men and women individually.

The breast is a source of nourishment for the dependent newborn. It is a reason to giggle for the pre-adolescent and a stumbling block of puzzlement and amazement for the developing teenager. For the young, sexual woman the breast is a sensuous and enticing link to her partner. For the expectant mother, its enlargement and engorgement indicate that a life is growing inside. The monthly tenderness that accompanies menstruation ties us to the other cycles of life and reminds us, just as the lunar cycles do, that we are ever evolving. With aging, our breasts, just like the other parts of our bodies, can no longer defy the laws of gravity and shift into new locations. While some parts of our bodies and our beings may seem frozen in place, time, and meaning, our breasts are our constant reminders that we are ever changing, both strong and vulnerable.

But as with so many things in our lives, we do not see them or appreciate them until they are forever altered or taken away. The wake-up call comes in that instant when a lump is found. In the moments that follow countless thoughts race through our heads. Is this for real? Could I be imagining this? Am I okay? What next? Who do I believe? What will become of me?

For the fortunate, answers to all the questions will come, as will the diagnosis that the mass is benign. These women can hold onto the message that there is nothing to worry about: Go home. Be assured. But stay vigilant.

For others the discovery is the first step into another world. The questions come faster than the answers, and the answers are only numbers and dosages and schedules and statistics and outcomes. The figures dance around us. But in moments of silence, when we look at ourselves and think our most private thoughts, we are met with the fact that the body—the body we have come to know, become comfortable with, and relied on—has changed. Has the breast turned on us and become an enemy from inside? Or has the diagnosis arrived in some Trojan horse? What is the cause? Why me? Why now?

The breast, the organ that defines us as sexual and reproductive creatures, is the focus of a battle. What started the war and how the story will end are as particular to each woman as the size and shape of each breast. There are guidelines but few roadmaps, and with breast cancer each path is singular.

Yet, if there was beauty and grace in the perfect, intact, sensuous breast, can there be beauty of a different sort in the breast that has been biopsied and cut and irradiated and poisoned? I think so. The human body is its own art form and is beautiful not only as it was created but also in the many shapes it takes on as it travels through life. Bodies with scars have not left the art behind. The scars simply mark the trail, the passage taken. Just like the moon and the sea and the fluctuating changes within us, the art of the altered breast is different but stays with us. Shocking? For some. Reassuring? For others.

Amelia Davis has painstakingly captured our forms and emotions, both sensuous and raw, through her bold eye. She has not backed away as so many of us have been urged to do. Through her photographs she challenges us: Look. See yourself in the mirror. Reacquaint yourself with the person within this altered house.

Even those of us who do not have breast cancer will see our sisters and mothers and girlfriends among these photographs. The images remind us of the female spirit's resilience and ring the bell calling all of us to unite in the circle of women. As with any circle, it is not complete until everyone, including the women featured in these pages, is drawn into it. The ties that join us are stronger than the cancers that try to pull us away from each other. There is much work to be done to bring us together. These pictures are our reminders.

preface

Breast cancer came knocking at my mother's door in 1993. My mother was already a veteran soldier, scarred and toughened by life. Eighteen years before my father had died of scleroderma. My mother lost the love of her life and faced the world alone with two small children. Then fourteen years later my mother collapsed on the bathroom floor. An ulcer had perforated and she was fighting for her life. She survived because she did not want to die.

Despite her abilities to face adversity, my mother was unprepared for the way she would look after a modified radical mastectomy—her only option—and how she would feel about herself. She and I tried to find pictures of what she would look like, but all we uncovered were pencil drawings of thin, flat, straight scars. Some women do end up looking like these pictures, but my mother—like the majority of women—did not. At sixty-seven years old, she was overweight and diabetic, so when her bandages came off for the first time in the hospital and she did not see what she expected, she felt mutilated and alone. I decided then that no woman should ever feel this way. All of my photography has been of a documentary nature, so I began to take photographs of women with breast cancer. My mother eagerly agreed to be the first subject. Since then I have been photographing women of all ages and ethnic backgrounds who are living with breast cancer.

I chose not to include the women's faces in these photographs for several reasons. In the beginning some women requested that their faces not be shown, and as time went on, I realized that their faces were unnecessary, even an impediment, to this project. The photographs are intended to let women see exactly what mastectomies, various types of reconstructive surgery, and lumpectomies look like, and I did not want to take the reader's attention away from that. Because today's society places so much emphasis on looks, the faces distracted from this purpose. I did not want any reader to look at these women and say, "She's old, she's young, she's pretty, she's ugly."

All these women invited me into their homes and shared a very intimate and personal part of their lives with me. Because I could photograph each woman in a setting of her choice, rather than in a studio with a backdrop, I was able to capture the individuality of each woman that a studio setting would erase. I also tried to use natural lighting whenever possible to give each photo more distinctiveness. One of my favorite photographers, Henri Cartier-Bresson, believed in the decisive moment. I tried to follow his philosophy of capturing the essence of the moment regardless of the lighting and the location of the subject. I hope readers will see and feel this moment when they look at the photographs.

It is important to me, not only as a photographer but also as a woman, to try to represent all women in this book because breast cancer does not discriminate. This disease affects women of all ages, all ethnic groups, and all socioeconomic backgrounds. Every woman has a voice and every woman should be heard. So readers could hear for themselves what these women thought and felt after their diagnoses, I have included narratives of their experiences. Most of these statements were written by the women and reflect what they wanted to say about cancer. I tried to maintain the power and integrity of their thoughts while smoothing the language and correcting grammar. A few of these pieces were written by me but are based on recordings or conversations. Since I met with these women over five years, the age listed for each is not current but instead refers to her age when the statement was composed. Some women wanted to be anonymous, so I used only first names or pseudonyms for all.

Fear of the unknown can be conquered only with knowledge. With this book in hand, women can eliminate their preconceived images of what breast cancer looks like and replace them with realities. Having visual representations of these realities removes the mystery and perhaps the fear. When a woman is diagnosed with breast cancer I hope she will pick up this book, flip through the photographs, read the women's stories, find someone she can relate to, and feel comfort in knowing that she is not alone.

Three months before my thirtieth birthday and three months before my mother's death, I was diagnosed with multiple sclerosis. Although I was faced with my own debilitating disease, I had the good fortune to spend my life with a truly courageous woman, my mother, and to spend years working with and talking with many other courageous women living with breast cancer. Though we do not share a disease, we do share an outlook on life. You never know what might hit you, but you face life head on with as much courage and dignity as possible. This is what I have learned from my photographic journey and this is the message I hope anyone faced with a disease will find in this book.

ACKNOWLEDGMENTS

*F*irst and foremost I would like to thank the incredible women featured in this book, for without them, there would be no book. You are an inspiration to us all. Thank you, Mom, Shevra, Rachel, Wanna, Betty, Charlotte, Ann, Noemi, Dorris, Marge, Barbara, Wanda, Susan, Lois, Carol, Wendy, Jennifer, Frances, Ruth, Raven Light, Annette, Merijane, Marleen, Maxine, Paula, and Andrée.

The First Look would not have been possible without an extremely generous grant from the William E. Weiss Foundation, Inc. Thank you for realizing the importance of and the need for this book and for taking a stand to make breast cancer visible rather than hidden. I am forever indebted to you. Special appreciation goes to Dwyer Brown and Fred Feldmesser for the instrumental roles they played in making the grant a reality.

Breast Cancer Action of San Francisco supported this book from the beginning and helped bring it to completion. Special thanks go to Barbara Brenner for her belief in me and her support.

Bonita Passarelli provided endless love and helped with every aspect of this book. I could not have done it without her. She is my strength.

When I was trying to find a publisher, Congresswoman Nancy Pelosi, Linda Ellerbee, Helen Crothers, and Dr. Dean Edell provided letters of praise for this project. I appreciate their efforts on my behalf.

Andrew Blauner, my agent, stuck with this book and believed in it when nobody else did. I'm lucky to have him. Jim Marshall went to bat for me with publishers and supported this book and my photography. I'm grateful for his friendship. Judy McCulloh, my editor at the University of Illinois Press, had the courage and foresight to know how much this book was needed. She embraced it instead of running from it.

Special thanks go to Nancy Snyderman for her contribution to the book and her never-ending and unquestioning help. Without Angie Bates, Nancy and I would never have connected. Loren Eskenazi and Saskia R. J. Thiadens not only wrote important contributions to the book but also offered support and friendship.

Whenever I needed help or had a question, Nancy Evans was always there and never asked for anything in return. She provided me with a list of resources, honest input, and advice.

Thanks go to Elizabeth A. Davis for being my sister and for having the brilliant idea of introducing me to Fred. I know Mom is proud of us.

I am grateful to Luis Penalver, who was patient and understanding with my family; Harriet Schatz, who got the ball rolling; and Kirk Anspach, who made the prints for all the photographs in this book. My friends and family were always there for me, and that helped me more than they will ever know.

This book is for my mother, but it is also for my friend Bena Duran and the women of the future.

To all of those who have helped me along the way but I have failed to acknowledge here, I apologize. Thank you, everyone.

. . . . *the first look* . . . .

Sheura

FORTY

I had my mastectomy three weeks before my wedding day. Two weeks after the surgery I went to the dressmaker to have my wedding dress refitted. While I was standing there one of my drainage wounds started to ooze. My dressmaker put a Band-aid on it and we went on with the fitting. I was thirty-three years old.

At the time I did not really question having reconstructive surgery, I just assumed I would do it. I went through three operations within the first year because I thought they would put me back together again. They helped me put off my reaction to losing my breast, but eventually that caught up with me. What I have now works fine under clothes and I'm used to it, but it's not a breast and it doesn't resemble what I lost. I even had to have cosmetic surgery on my healthy breast so that it would look more like my reconstructed "breast." If I had it to do over, I don't know whether I would choose reconstructive surgery.

Four years after the mastectomy I learned that the cancer had spread to my lung. I had more surgery followed by chemotherapy. This surgery left me with chronic pain and the complications from the chemotherapy nearly killed me. My husband spent sleepless nights with me in the hospital because he was afraid I would die and he did not want me to die alone. In addition, I lost my hair, suffered extreme weight loss, and developed lymphedema. Eventually my hair grew back and I regained most of the weight I had lost, but I'll have to deal with the lymphedema for the rest of my life. It's harder to hide than a mastectomy.

There were other side effects, too. At first I could not get pregnant; then I was told I should not get

1

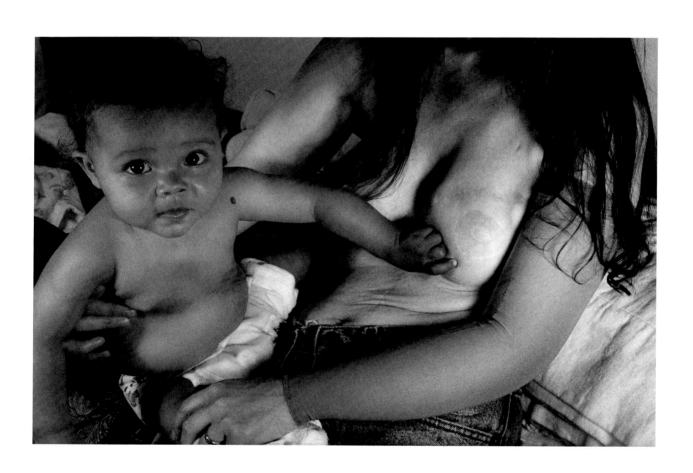

pregnant. The pain of this information was over-whelming, but it subsided when we adopted our baby girl. I don't think about biological children anymore, just as I don't question what my marriage—or my life—would have been like without cancer. In spite of it, or maybe because of it, I seem to have more love in my life than most people do.

My husband and I have been living with breast cancer for all of our married life. He says that seeing my first mammogram, which showed a tumor with spidery tendrils radiating through my breast, was far worse for him than my mastectomy scar. When I told him I was going to pose for this book he said, "You should. You're beautiful."

I'm doing okay now, although my health is fragile. I'm on tamoxifen, which has side effects I don't like, but I can't take any risks because my chances of hav-ing another recurrence are extremely high. I know the cancer can and probably will spread. If it shows up in my other breast I'll feel lucky; a breast is more expendable than a brain.

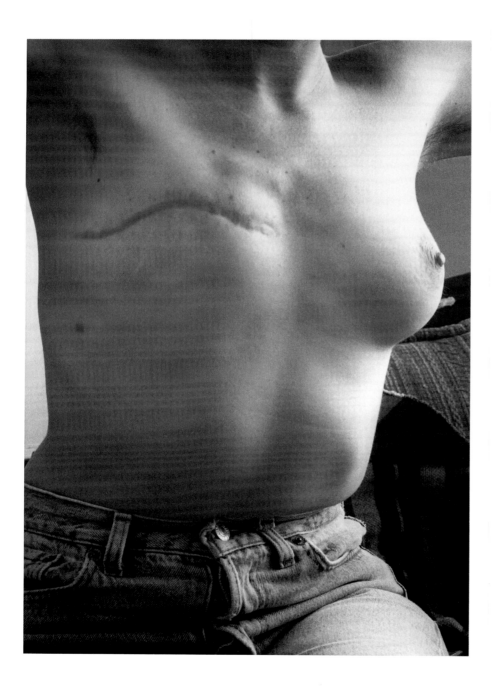

Rachel

Here it is, "the scar," four months after surgery—a graphic symbol of breast cancer hell. Interestingly, although the disease is a major concern for women, most of us have never seen the results of breast surgery—especially a mastectomy scar. Posing for this book, taking a shower in a locker room, even wearing a bathing suit is sort of like "coming out." Some women are frightened by the sight of the scar and look away, while others openly appreciate the bravery of those women who are willing to show what they look like after surgery.

Sometimes when I look at my scar, I feel sorry for myself and think, Why me? Why do I have to be a statistical anomaly? I am an otherwise healthy twenty-eight-year-old with breast cancer. Other times I see the scar as a battle wound, a positive symbol of my survival, perseverance, and strength. Having undergone a mastectomy has made me love my body more than ever. Like most women, I'd always been neurotic about my weight, the size of my butt, my hair, etc. Now when I look at myself in the mirror, I simply love my body for what it is and I'm thankful for being alive.

Numerous physicians have urged me to reconsider reconstructive surgery because I am so young. But I don't plan on having reconstruction and don't even wear a prosthesis. This "do nothing" option is one seldom discussed by doctors. I strongly feel that my mastectomy is inextricably part of who I am now, and I don't want to hide that from the world. For better or worse, breast cancer has changed my life forever. I live with the constant, nagging fear of recurrence, but I also draw on the strength that fear gives me when setting priorities in my life and interacting with everyone around me. In a convoluted way, this experience has strengthened my self-esteem and personal confidence. Indeed, if I can effectively confront the daily challenges of living with breast cancer, then I can do almost anything.

Wanna

I learned about "titty sickness" when I was about nine years old. Someone was teasing my friend about her mother. She said that Miss Agnes had the "titty sickness" and the doctors had dug out all of her titty meat—she had a hole in her chest. When we told Miss Agnes about the teasing she pulled down her T-strap dress and showed us her chest. It was a gruesome sight for nine-year-olds and I never forgot it. She laughed and said, "I may be ugly, but I'm alive."

Over the next few years two of my great-aunts came back home to New Iberia, Louisiana, from Texas, suffering from that same "titty sickness." Miss Agnes helped Mom and Mother take care of them until they died.

Twenty-five years later when I was diagnosed, "titty sickness" had a new name—breast cancer. I was told that I was lucky because even though they had cut off my breast, I wouldn't have a hole in my chest and I would live. I thought about Miss Agnes and decided that I could always laugh and use her line: "I may be ugly, but I'm alive."

Twenty years ago breast reconstruction was not covered by my insurance and the "flesh-colored" prosthesis was not the color of my flesh. When a law was passed to make reconstruction a right, my doctor said he didn't recommend it but would do it if I insisted. He put me on a twenty-four-month waiting list. I then went to a black female plastic surgeon because I hoped she would understand and could minimize the keloid scarring. But the scars, especially on my inner thigh, are ugly. I stopped the process because it only seemed to make things worse. Besides, I had no hole in my chest.

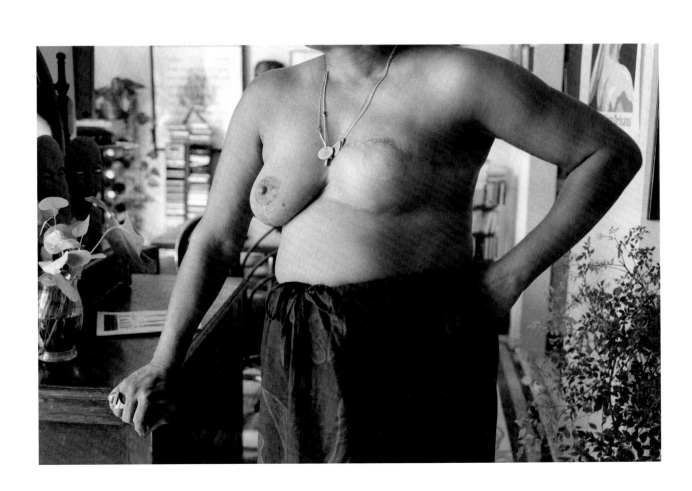

For the past eighteen years I have been an advocate for all women, especially poor women, living with and dying from this disease. As a twenty-year survivor, women look to me for support and hope that they, too, will be long-term survivors.

I wrote and published the following poem entitled "Alive to Testify" and that is also the title of my book of "story poems." These "story poems" are about the pain and joy experienced by poor women and women of color who have been afflicted with this disease. The poem speaks to mainstream breast cancer organizations about the daily challenges faced in poor communities.

Alive to Testify

I's got to reach out to keep 'um alive
din you kin teach 'um to testify
'bout da air an da watus
dat's killin' us daughtus.

So pleas don't dis me 'caus my ribbons' pink
I wears it to make my sista's think (more soft)
'bout breakin down barriers, 'bout choosin life
   (more soft)
'bout early detection—maybe even da knife.

We's got problem's you don't know
we shedin layers, we tryin' to grow
to trust—to believe—to claim our power
to save lives lost hour after hour.

We hafta save lives one at a time
we's got to catch up—we's behind
so save us a place, we's on our way
getting stronga ev'ry day by day.

We's makin it known, makin it unda-stood
soon no toxins/dioxins a-llowed in da Hood
but first we's got to stay alive—
din we will stand—(wid you) to testify.

My message, my mission, my ministry is that early detection saves lives. It is natural to fear this disease, but we can use that fear to propel us to action.

Betty

June 24, 1994—a day etched in my mind and heart forever. I left the breast clinic in a daze; everything was spinning around me. To this day, I have no idea how I drove home.

I remember my doctor telling me how sorry he was for me and I remember responding that I was upset and angry. The best way I can relate my experiences is to introduce you to SARAH. It is not unusual to have a visit from her, which may last just a few hours or maybe several days, sometime in one's life.

SHOCK My first reaction was pure and simple shock: I am healthy. I have no lumps. This could not be happening to me.

ANGER The next day I became quite angry: This is not fair! Why me? I do not deserve this (who does?).

There are still many things I want to experience and accomplish and places I want to see.

REJECTION Soon my anger turned to rejection: There has been a mistake. The reports/results are not mine. This is a bad dream. Tomorrow morning when I awake this will be over.

ACCEPTANCE When I met with the surgeon two days later, I was beginning to accept that I had breast cancer and was ready to understand the options and educate myself about this disease.

HOPE I quickly came to realize that I indeed was fortunate. I had early stage microcalcifications (no lumps) that had been detected on my annual mammogram. The treatment plan I chose was

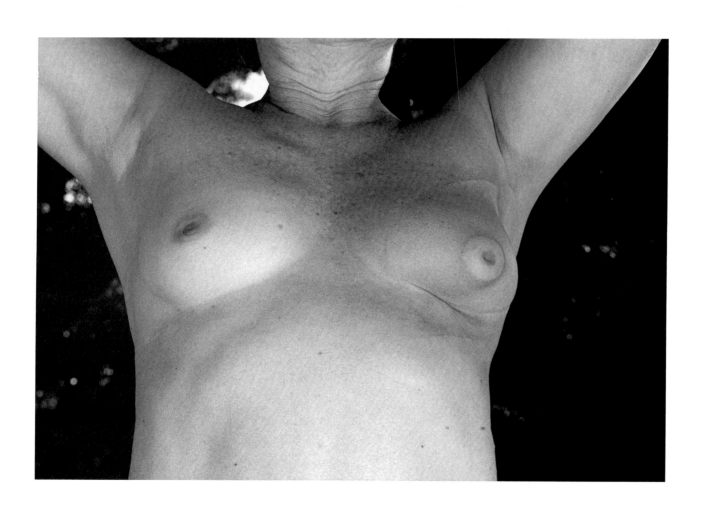

lumpectomy with radiation. With early detection, a great medical team, and supportive family and friends, I have hope for a long healthy life.

The road to recovery has had its ups and downs, but I have grown as a person through this ordeal. I reorganized my life by resetting priorities, recognizing what is important, and letting go of relationships that were superficial. At the same time, I worked on improving those relationships that have value.

I could not have done as well as I have without the support of family, friends, and doctors who are always there for me. My husband, Bob, is a constant support both emotionally and physically. He encourages me to smile, to laugh, to exercise, and to maintain contact with friends. Also, it is reassuring to talk with breast cancer survivors. The sharing of experiences, whether in an informal network or a support group, is comforting. There is a big sisterhood out there ready to help. By contributing to this effort, I hope that I may help someone through a rough time.

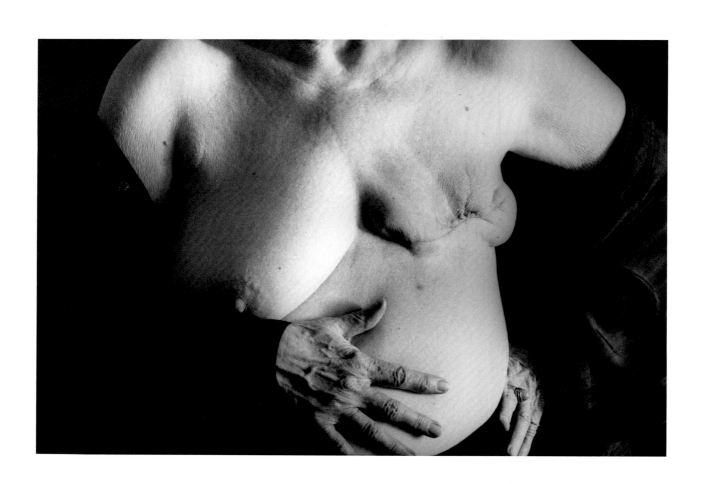

Mom

Late in the afternoon on a Thursday in June, I walked into an operating room, hoisted myself up onto a table, stretched out, and was told to breathe deeply. All I remember is that the operating room was tiled in depressing shades of green. Of the anesthetic, of the modified radical mastectomy, I remember nothing. During the very early hours of the following day, I was nauseous and kept waking and sleeping. Midmorning, the surgeon came in smiling. He asked if I had looked at the wound (a word used by doctors, who never say *cut*). I told him I hadn't, but that I'd felt along my left side and found a long, thick, lumpy caterpillar. "Let's take a look," he said as he opened my hospital gown and, without warning, pulled the Coverderm tape across and off my chest in one smooth motion. That was a shock. I was more shocked when he told me there were no stitches, there would be no dressing, and the ten staples (the lumps of the caterpillar I'd felt) would adequately

hold the wound and would be removed in a week. The surgeon took the time to reassure me that many women don't want to see the mastectomy site the first few days. I didn't look until the following day when I was home, alone in the bathroom, some forty-odd hours after my left breast and twenty-four axillary lymph nodes had been removed.

My scar hasn't changed much since I first dared look. It doesn't bother me, and I'm not disturbed that I have only one breast. As soon as I felt that large lump on the underside of my left breast I knew it would have to come off. When I learned that my breast cancer was stage 3, I was prepared to accept surgery as the only option. And when asked if I wanted to consider reconstruction later, I said no without any hesitation. I had nursed two daughters so I believed the breast had served me, and them, well. My age and that I've been a widow for seventeen years were factors in that decision. Another determinant was my own style. I don't like confining, restrictive clothing; I haven't worn a bra for many years and one would be necessary if I chose to use most of the kinds of available prostheses. And so, no reconstruction and no prosthesis. I don't mind being lop-sided.

According to the advice I received from a medical oncologist after the surgery and according to the books and articles I'd read prior to my mastectomy, chemotherapy is not the recommended treatment for a postmenopausal woman with breast cancer the size of mine. The medical oncologist advised radiation to lower the odds of breast cancer recurring in the same site, and I've gone along with her counsel.

During the six-week period of radiation treatment, I did not feel ill at all. Only time will tell whether the 5,040 rads helped my body fight off the cancer.

I have just one other comment for those women who, like me, are not very stoic. It is true that there is no pain in the mastectomy area after surgery, so please don't worry about that. And please don't worry about how you'll look. We must make informed choices to save our lives, not our looks.

My mother, Maxine, survived breast cancer but died from a ruptured aortic aneurysm in 1998.

Charlotte

It was almost a relief to be diagnosed with breast cancer. I had spent twenty-five years feeling lumps in my fibrocystic breasts and worrying through countless doctor's examinations and mammograms. All those years I wondered if I would end up looking like my grandmother or my mother, both of whom had no breasts and horrible scars and both of whom had died in their forties from breast cancer. I was relieved that my cancer was detected early, that mastectomy scars don't have to look like my mother's, and that with chemotherapy my chances for recovery are 85 percent. My mother and grandmother never had the options I'd been given. I felt I could take a different road—a road to recovery rather than certain death.

My husband first noticed that my left nipple became inverted when I raised my arm. In hindsight, I should have insisted on a biopsy then instead of waiting for two years because the mammogram was negative. When the cancer was confirmed, I decided to have a double mastectomy—I had done research on prophylactic mastectomies because of my family history. I also decided to have immediate reconstruction with tissue expanders. These were later replaced by saline implants. After the first surgery, I found it hard to look at myself, but I never experienced the feeling of "no breasts."

Even though I was pleased with my new breasts, they did not look like those on the slides my husband had seen before the surgery, and this became a constant battle between us. After numerous operations to correct size differences, encapsulations, and even a ruptured implant, I finally gathered enough courage to have the "big" operation, the TRAM flap, which I had been told about in the beginning. As a result of this major operation—where the fat on the abdomen is

transferred under the skin and used as new breast tissue—I now have two soft, warm, natural-looking breasts instead of two large, firm mounds on my chest. My husband thinks I look sexy again. My friends who politely told me earlier how great I looked now all agree that I look 100 percent better.

After all those years of being afraid of my breasts (all those precancerous lumps), of considering my breasts to be milk factories (four children), of thinking my breasts were too large (34 DD), and three years of experiencing hard "implant breasts," I now feel happier, sexier, and better looking than ever. And now, to my children's embarrassment, when I feel hungry, I rub my breasts and say, "I'm starving."

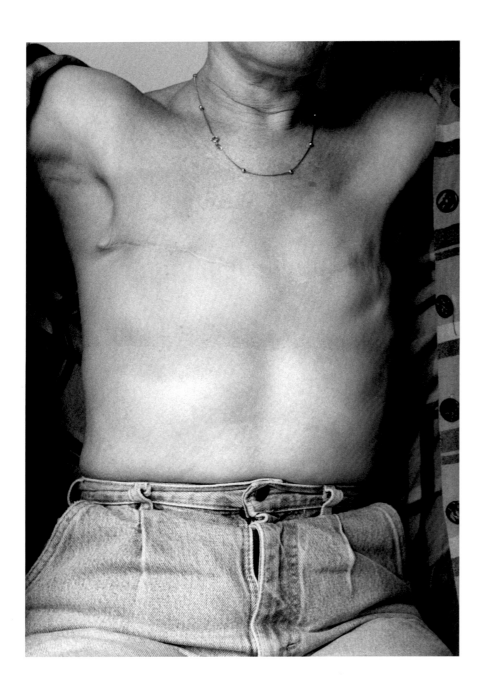

Ann

I was in a state of shock when I learned that the lump I had discovered in my breast was cancerous. No one in my immediate group of family, friends, and co-workers had prepared me to expect that this could happen to me. In 1985, breast cancer was just beginning to be talked about as an epidemic and that did help me to accept the diagnosis. To cope, I proceeded with the tests and made the decision in a "can-do" but almost trancelike mode.

The surgeon I saw was progressive and felt each patient was in charge of her treatment. For me, the issue was survival; the mastectomy and its disfigurement were secondary. I was thankful I was forty years old, that I had already questioned the issue of body image as the key to a woman's acceptance in our society, and that I could accept my new form after the mastectomy. I knew that reconstruction was an option I could exercise anytime, and that comforted me.

The lump I found eight years later in my remaining breast, despite my adherence to doctor's visits and follow-up mammograms, made me angry and fearful. Again, for me, the mastectomy was secondary. This time, I felt I was really facing my own mortality. The fact that nodes were involved put me into a different category and the treatment I needed involved a lengthy, complex plan. Working with a new surgeon, other doctors, and a myriad of medical people challenged me constantly to feel in charge of my life overall.

As a survivor of breast cancer and two mastectomies, I am still being challenged every day.

Noemi

My life changed when I found out I had breast cancer. At first, I thought my life was over. I was very scared because I didn't know what to do and felt so alone. I wondered if my husband was strong enough to cope with this problem. I wondered who would help me. At the age of twenty-six, I had a mastectomy, went through chemotherapy, and almost lost my husband during the process. Then, a year later, I had a bone marrow transplant. During chemotherapy, I cried when my hair fell out. When I put on extra weight, I felt like a giant pig. I kept asking my husband if he still loved the way I looked. Although he reassured me that I would lose the weight after the treatment, month after month I continued to gain. I was fat and bald but I wouldn't let myself think I was ugly. I started putting more makeup on and made sure the wigs I wore looked like natural hair. I told myself that no one could help me except myself. I got through it.

The bone marrow transplant was not an easy procedure. At first, I was skeptical and scared. I had to wait because the insurance company denied preauthorization, claiming that the treatment was experimental. When the process did start, I had to stay in the hospital for thirty days while my marrow was harvested. It was the most painful process I had been through. I tried to keep up a positive attitude by wearing regular clothes in order to feel like a normal, healthy person. To me, hospital clothes are only for sick people and I never considered myself ill. Every afternoon I walked around the hospital lobby twenty times and then, before I went to bed at night, I rode a stationary bike. During that month, I was not allowed to go out of the building for fresh air. I felt like I was incarcerated without having committed any crime.

After the bone marrow transplant, I tried to pick up where I had left off but things were different. Every-

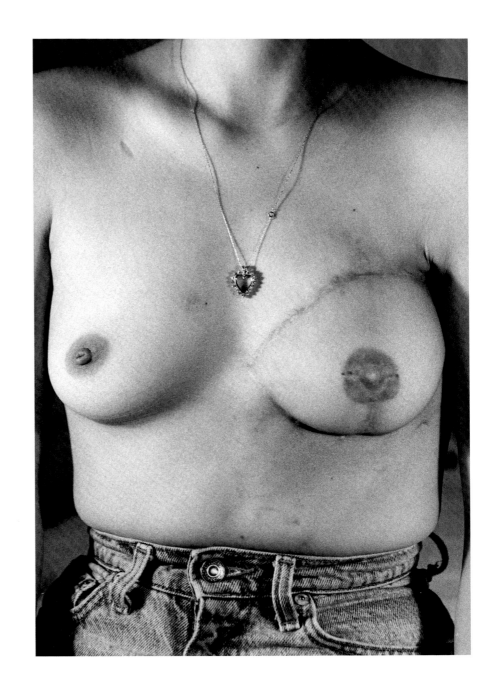

thing seemed changed somehow. I didn't know what was wrong until I found out my husband was having an affair. I was crushed. I hated myself and didn't want to live anymore. My husband told me the reason he turned his back on me was my inability to bear a child. This was very painful; my heart was shattered into little pieces. Then he compared me to his girlfriend, telling me about her nice, gorgeous body and big breasts. I hated my life during that moment. But I said to myself, I will have a breast again and I will make sure it is the prettiest breast in the whole world. After I spoke to my oncologist, I met with a specialist and had reconstructive surgery. I remember that, as I woke up after the surgery, the first thing that came out of my mouth was "I have a breast now." I didn't have to worry anymore about a prosthesis sagging or shifting. I lost my breast, but I got it back. I am very confident and proud.

SIXTY-SIX

On October 23, 1982, I found out that I had breast cancer. I had a dream that was so real—they removed the lump and I was okay. It was early morning and I woke up and put my hand right on the lump. I went to work, called Kaiser, and got an emergency appointment.

When I got to Kaiser on Geary Street, a nurse practitioner was assigned to me. She did a routine examination and was not able to feel the lump. So she asked me very sarcastically, What makes you think you have a lump? I had already explained the dream to her, so I simply said, Would you like me to put your hands on it? and I did. Immediately she dashed out of the room. When she came back she told me I would need to have a biopsy right away.

Dr. Jackson came into the waiting area and his shoulders were all the way down—you could tell that he had bad news that he did not want to give. So I made it a little bit easier for him. Because of the dream I knew I was going to be all right. I said to him, "It's malignant, right?" and he said yes.

I asked all kinds of questions. I asked him what his procedure would be, what kind of surgery he was talking about. When he said a mastectomy, I asked why. He explained to me that small tumors could be growing and there would be no way for him to see them, so this was the safest and best operation. It was a precaution.

Dr. Jackson called in Dr. Hendrixson. They talked to me for about an hour. Neither one was able to convince me that my breast needed to come off. So I said to the two of them, If you find cancer in my lymph nodes and other places, you have permission to take my breast off. But if you find only

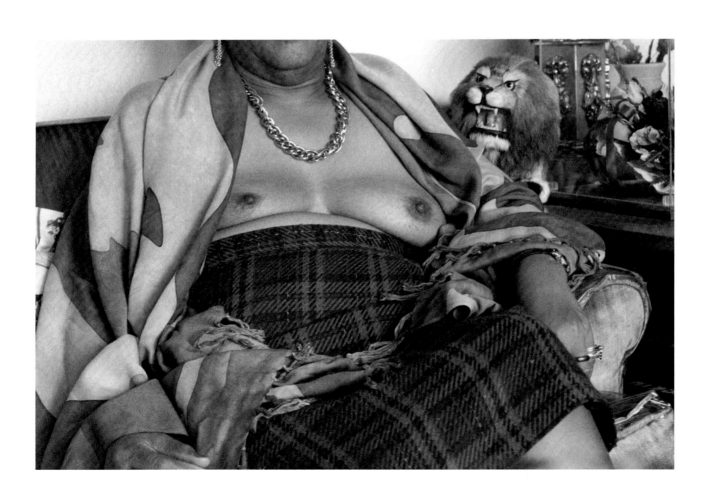

this lump, then remove just the lump. They agreed to do that.

Dr. Jackson met me in the recovery room and he said I was lucky. I said no, I was blessed. They had planned to do chemotherapy first and then radiation, but because they were quite sure they had removed all of the tumor and there was no sign of cancer in any of the lymph nodes, they reversed the treatment. My radiation treatment caused my skin to be about fifteen times darker than it had been. It took about three years for the color to lighten and look more like the rest of me. The breast was hard to the touch—not hard like a brick, but it was *hard*. As the color came back and the softness came back, it became much smaller then my left breast.

I never had a single pain pill, I never had any hair loss, and I never lost any food, even though everything smelled awful. The chemotherapy goes through your system and makes your skin and your clothing and your bedding smell terrible. I don't care how much you wash or what perfumes you use, you still have that awful odor on your skin.

I do believe that if we have a positive outlook on our situation, if we can just know and believe that we're going to be fine, everything is going to turn out okay for us. I think that's 90 percent of the battle. I also believe that with new technology we'll have fewer women who will lose their lives, especially if they're bold enough to go and not sit around and let things get out of control. I realize that we won't always be able to find our tumors through breast examination—I examined my breasts, but I never felt that lump and neither did the nurse practitioner. It took the Lord showing it to me through a dream to know that I had it and was at risk.

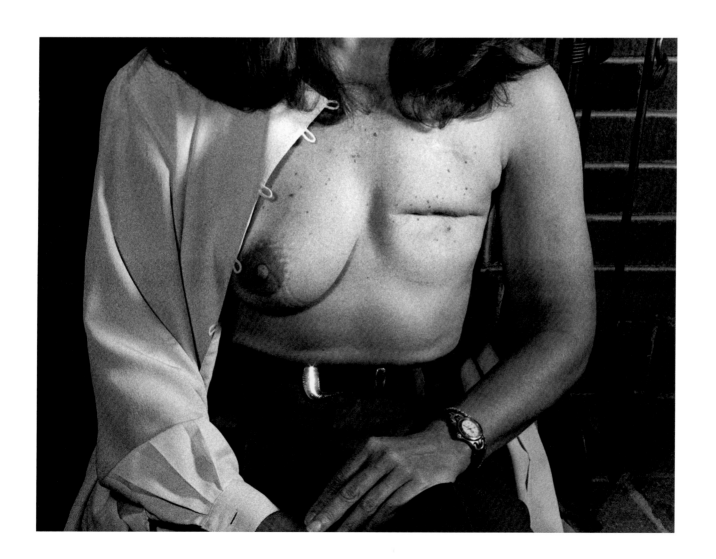

Marge

When I first discovered I had cancer, I was very angry with my body. I was in great shape—good health, eating well—and I felt my body had betrayed me. At some point the anger was replaced by shame because my body no longer mirrored the image that society expects of us. I spent three years alone, feeling unwanted, unloved, and ashamed, yet craving the touch of another human. I isolated myself because I felt "less than" everyone else.

I have learned to love my body and myself as I am. I am a beautiful person inside and out and I am prepared to give and receive love. I have discovered that people see my scar as a badge of courage and love me more for having survived the battle. I have given myself my life to enjoy and live to its fullest. No longer will I separate myself from others. We all have scars, but some are more visible than others.

Barbara

FIFTY-EIGHT

In 1984, after fifteen years of careful, ongoing breast examinations because of fibrocystic disease, a mammogram detected a tumor in my right breast. It was malignant and twenty-seven of thirty lymph nodes were positive. I opted to have a lumpectomy, radiation, and chemotherapy instead of a mastectomy since it had just been determined that this less aggressive therapy was equally effective.

I love life and I felt I still had much to accomplish, so I took charge of my recovery. Along with the invaluable support of a marvelous team of doctors who (as they told me later) believed at the time that I had little chance of surviving, we went to war with the cancer. Between 1985 and 1988 we took several biopsies in response to questionable mammogram readings. Eventually we found microscopic malignant tissue in the other breast. At the urging of all six of my doctors plus two others we consulted, I had

bilateral mastectomies. It was a difficult decision but I knew it was the only way I could get beyond the endless chain of mammograms and biopsies and the constant dread of what negative results might mean.

I hated my body and the prostheses even though I knew I had made the right decision. In 1990 I had reconstructive breast surgery—one side took an implant but the side that had been irradiated could not, so I had a breast created from abdominal muscle and tissue. This had to be altered the following year because the radiation damage prevented normal healing. Then I developed lymphedema in my right arm.

The man with whom I had a relationship of several years was unable to deal with this (or any) illness, so we parted. (He died recently of congestive heart failure at age sixty-two and *I* was at *his* funeral.) The cancer made me feel damaged and a bad risk for any

future relationship. I still am not comfortable with my body. I don't like the way it looks or feels. I've gained forty pounds from medication, the edema, and overeating. I am not pleased when I look in the mirror or at photographs. I wonder if I'll ever have another relationship with a man.

I have been blessed throughout this struggle with loving support from family and friends and a career that I love. I also feel very lucky to be alive, strong, and healthy after ten years and against all the odds. I have a full, rich life with many friends and many interests. I have a lot to do and I intend to keep on, hopefully for many more years.

Barbara died of breast cancer in 1995.

Wanda

had a problem with my bra. I thought, Maybe my breast is changing to a different shape or something because I had seven kids. So I went to the doctor and he told me that I had a tumor and it had to be removed.

Mom was absent. She couldn't give me advice. I blocked my family out of my life because when I got diagnosed with cancer, nobody came toward me. They sent me flowers and a bunch of cards in the mail.

I was freaked out—really scared. I said, Well, I'm going to get a second opinion, because now you say you're going to have to cut me. No, this can't be happening. So I went for a second opinion. He did a mammogram—see, I never had a mammogram done. He read the results to me. He said, "Yes, you have a tumor on your left breast. It's the size of an orange and it has to be removed."

I had my seventh child when I discovered that I had breast cancer. I was twenty-eight and finishing a drug recovery program. I was going through it for two years and maintaining my household and making sure my health was my number one priority—trying to let go of my job for a moment, then going back to work. It was a big struggle for me.

I got a bunch of literature on cancer because I didn't know anything about cancer. They said that it was in my lymph nodes on my left side and I would have to go through this procedure and have them removed. So, I got all the literature—I called everything in the phone book, anything that had to deal with cancer.

My doctor wrote me a prescription to smoke marijuana because—now get this—it helped me enhance my eating capacity. I couldn't hold food down. When I went through chemo I lost seventy-some pounds.

I was getting a prescription to smoke marijuana, and I was in a drug program.

I had no insurance, no benefits, no nothing, but because I was living with Big Larry, we weren't on welfare. He works and was paying for everything—I wasn't eligible for anything. That left me penniless the whole eighteen months that I was in my program.

Going through cancer, I had picked up a little skill of making hats—fashion hats. It was something I wanted to give back to the community. I lost all my hair, so I got into hats—I thought I could pass it on to other women.

I reached out—just talked to people and connected with lots of programs that help you, sharing and talking with other women about what I experienced, what I'm going through, and what made them strong. It made me feel like I had something to hold onto because these women were looking forward to me coming and sharing my stories. I went way across town because I didn't want people from my side of town to see me. I felt stripped of something, and on the other side of town none of the people knew me.

I'm a black woman from the Bayview Hunters Point area and at a lot of the support groups I went to nobody was black and I was the youngest. I couldn't get loose because there are certain kinds of things you say around people like you—you feel more at ease. But I looked in their eyes and I was the same as them.

Based on excerpts from Wanda's interview for the Breast Cancer Oral History Action Project.

Susan

Ever since Susan was diagnosed and treated for a recurrence of her primary breast cancer, she has spent all of her (limited) energy on advocacy. At the time the manuscript for this book was being prepared, Susan had temporarily relocated to Houston, Texas, to take over as the volunteer director for the Seventh Biennial Symposium on Minorities, the Medically Underserved, and Cancer. The symposium is sponsored by the Intercultural Cancer Council, the nation's largest multicultural and multidisciplinary coalition addressing the unequal burden of cancer in minority and medically underserved communities in the United States and its territories. Susan was working with a skeleton team of dedicated staff and volunteers for twenty hours per day on average. Susan was close to exhaustion and physically and emotionally unable to write. Susan shared some of her thoughts with me at the time of our photo shoot, and they inform the following narrative.

It was important for Susan to include her dog in the photograph because Zack is also a recurrent cancer survivor. In fact, Susan believes that pet therapy and her advocacy work are two key factors in her survival (when her recurrence was diagnosed she was given only ten months to live).

Susan was first diagnosed with breast cancer in 1991 at the age of thirty-four. She was doing well until late 1996, when she suddenly developed unilateral weakness and numbness, acute lumbar pain, severe headaches, and chronic nausea. In January 1997 she was diagnosed with carcinomatous meningitis, in which cancer spreads to the cerebral spinal fluid. Once she completed treatment, her left-sided weakness all but disappeared, but Susan was left with severe, intractable lumbar pain. She is now being treated as a chronic pain patient, receiving twenty-four-hour narcotics through an infusion pump and intradermal

patches. Unfortunately, the narcotics work only well enough to take the edge off her pain and leave her groggy and tired (another reason why Susan had difficulty writing about herself). Although she is in constant pain, she tries not to let this interfere with her advocacy work.

Since Susan is a third-generation Japanese American (Sansei), she is particularly interested in bringing public awareness to Asian and Pacific Islander women about their risk for breast cancer. When she went to her doctor with a prominent lump back in 1991, Susan's surgeon told her that she was too young to have breast cancer and that "Asian women don't get breast cancer." She takes her message of advocacy to the medical and research communities and state legislators. As founder of the Asian and Pacific Islander National Cancer Survivors Network and chair of the Intercultural Cancer Council, Susan's message is also reaching Congress and the White House.

Susan views her mastectomy scar as a badge of honor. Although she would never wish breast cancer on anyone, she feels that having had cancer was both the worst and the best thing that ever happened to her. She hopes her photograph and those of the other women in this book will lessen the fear of what breast cancer looks like. Having met her husband three years after her mastectomy, Susan wants to assure women that losing a breast does not take away one's beauty, strength, sexuality, or sensuality. It's the beauty on the inside that made her husband, Rob, fall in love with her. Susan told me, "No one can take that away from you." I think she's right.

Lois

I was thirty-one years old and happily married with a one-year-old son when I discovered a lump in my right breast. I thought I was in good health: I had no outward physical signs of cancer; I felt no pain; no other family member had ever had breast cancer— certainly not my sisters or my mother. I remember lying in bed very relaxed when a voice told me to feel under my right arm. My fingers went to the exact spot and I felt a lump.

When I was diagnosed with breast cancer, I felt like I had run headfirst into a brick wall. I had always thought that cancer and death were synonymous. I felt numb, like I was on automatic pilot. So, I entrusted myself to my doctors' care and let them guide me. They gave me one choice: a modified radical mastectomy. I was diagnosed on a Thursday and on Monday of the following week my right breast was gone.

Today, my biggest regret is that I allowed myself to be rushed into having a mastectomy. I should have taken the time to get a second opinion. I should have asked some basic questions: What kind of cancer did I have? Did I need a mastectomy? What other procedures were available? What would I look like after a mastectomy? Will a mastectomy mean the loss of my sexuality, my husband's love? I should have contacted a breast cancer hotline, a local women's health group, or simply another woman with breast cancer. We owe it to ourselves to be informed before surgery so that we, not the doctors, can decide what is best for us.

Fortunately, I can honestly say that sex was not a problem. Although at first we tried to pretend that there was no difference in my body, my husband convinced me that my having only one breast did not matter. The time I felt most vulnerable, however, was when I was fully recuperated physically and ready to

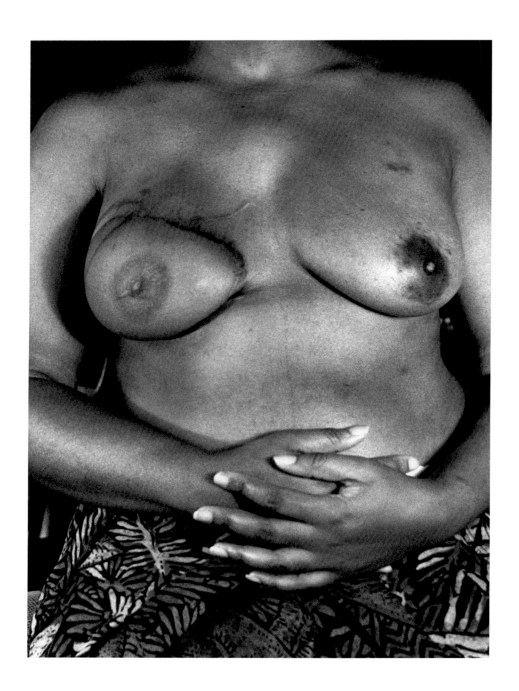

go back to work. Nothing I had read prepared me for shopping for a prosthesis. It was hard to have people taking my measurements, bringing out different shapes and sizes, trying to find something that looked natural on me when all the prostheses are pink and I am a black woman. I even had to change my style of clothing from T-shirts and sweaters to oversized blouses.

Two years after my mastectomy, I decided I wanted something that was more like my breast; I was tired of a prosthesis that slipped out of place. I decided upon breast reconstruction. This time, I didn't rush. After investigating the different methods of reconstruction and the kinds of surgeries available, I chose to have a silicon implant. Although the implant was slightly smaller than my other breast, I didn't feel unbalanced, but I did have to compensate somewhat by stuffing the implant side more. Some years later, I started having chest pains. I did not really know if the pains were related to the silicon implant, but decided it would be a good thing for the implant to go. I thought I would just have to live with nothing again. That's when I met a doctor who referred me to a reconstructive surgeon. I was impressed with the pictures of her work, so that is the route I took. Now, I don't care about my scars: when people look, there is something there. I am able to say that I had breast cancer and these scars are the result. I couldn't do that before.

It's taken me twelve years to feel completely satisfied with my body, just as it has taken me twelve years to find out what is really important to me. My experience has allowed me to search deep into my soul and to strengthen my spirituality. Crises can be painful but transformation is rarely possible without them.

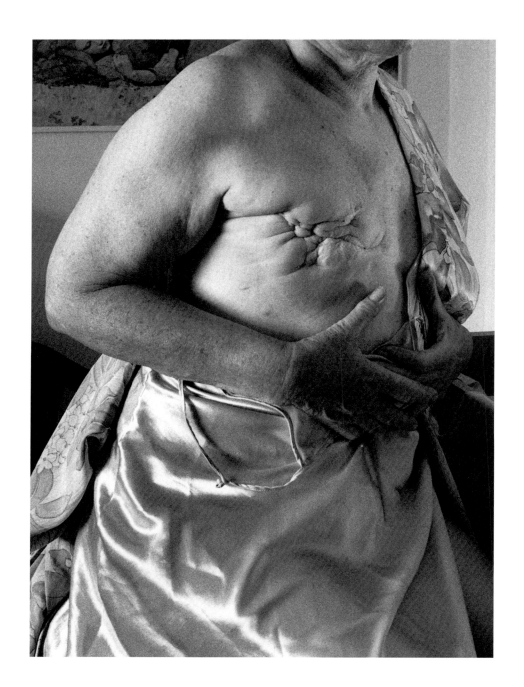

Carol

SEVENTY

*V*oila! Here's the pathetic but slightly comical remnant of what was once my right breast. Thanks to a fine prosthesis and a pretty bra, nobody sees it naked like this. To me, it looks like a couple of cartoon characters having an altercation. I didn't expect that. I imagined a flat, blank area of skin with maybe a line of scar across it.

I found the lump myself and from the moment of discovery to my return home from the surgery only three weeks passed—too little for me to assimilate the implications and impact of cancer and mastectomy on myself and my family. I'm still not used to this weird scene on my front. I may live to be one hundred and still be surprised by my one-sidedness.

My surgeon forewarned me that I would be numb in my upper arm and right breast area for six months and that I would experience twinges or discomfort (he didn't say "pain") for six months after that. I think my emotional course is following the same schedule. Three months post-surgery, I am still numb, but grateful that I made it through without more infection, more cancer, radiation, or chemo. I take two tamoxifen a day as prevention and precaution.

The whole experience was less horrendous then I had always imagined. I'm still here.

41

Wendy

TWENTY-FIVE

My gynecologist found a lump in my left breast a few weeks after my twenty-third birthday. My parents had given me health insurance as a college graduation present and I was trying to be responsible. I had my first real job teaching environmental education and was proud to be independent. I wasn't worried about the lump because my mother has had several benign lumps removed. I was sure it would be nothing and didn't want to have it removed in what I knew would be an expensive waste of time. My gynecologist was not convinced. She calmly told me to take up my arguments with a surgeon that she recommended. So, full of cynicism and resentment, I went to the surgeon. He was patient with me even when I all but accused him of recommending unnecessary surgery to line his pockets. He spoke to me quietly and explained that I had no choice. When I told him that I didn't make enough money to pay for surgery he said that he would do it for free, but it had

to be done. Looking back, I think that was when I first considered that there might be something seriously wrong with me.

I had the biopsy the day before Thanksgiving so I wouldn't miss work. Two weeks later I went to get the results. I was busy and preoccupied. I was going to stop briefly by the doctor's office and then make good use of the rest of my day off by running a whole list of errands. I remember feeling relieved on the drive to his office. Now all this would be over. We met in his office again and the first thing he said to me was, "It's not nothing." It took a minute for the information to sink in. Throughout the rest of the conversation my mind was spinning, slipping in and out of gear. I remember discussing abnormal cell growth, reconstructive surgery, and an appointment at the Stanford Medical Center and thinking about the picture behind his desk of him wearing bright Gortex

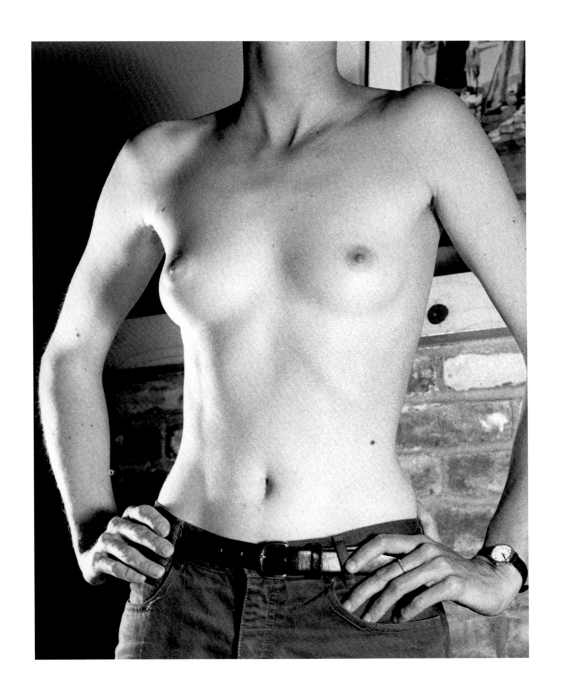

while standing on top of a snow-covered peak. The rest of the day was a blur. I told my housemate, Stephanie, I told my boss, I told Adam, and finally that evening I told my parents.

Somehow the next few months passed. I worked two and sometimes three jobs and paid my bills. I read some about cancer, but mostly I tried not to think about what might happen. Most of my friends were great. My ex-boyfriend drove two hours out of his way to clean up the mess that my housemates had left when they flew home for Christmas, Mrs. Glynn stayed up late talking to me about life and cooked me pepper soup, Jo Crane called me from the East Coast to talk to me about her breast cancer, and through it all Adam and my parents took care of me.

There were some people, however, who just didn't understand. Some of my older co-workers would corner me with questions I couldn't answer, questions about why I had cancer. I must have done something, they implied. Had I been thinking bad thoughts, holding in my anger, eating the wrong foods? I learned to recognize these people and devised a defense. I would compose my face into a properly penitent expression and say, "Oh, well, I ate a ton of peanut butter when I was a kid. Aflatoxins, you know." This seems to comfort people. It sounds scientific and they can say to themselves, "I never really liked peanut butter. I must be safe. I won't get cancer."

I eventually had a lumpectomy and have been free of cancer for seven years. I am three years into a Ph.D. program at UC–Davis and am making plans for a healthy future. If I am sick again I will do some things differently—I will get more second opinions and let my friends and family help more. I have done more research, I get mammograms every year, and my life is more stable.

Jennifer

Here I am five weeks after surgery. Soon I will have the nipple tattooed on my reconstructed breast to match the color of the other one.

It all began in early February 1994 when I noticed a clear discharge coming from my right nipple. I had the same feeling that I'd had when I was a nursing mother and made an appointment for an immediate examination. At that time, samples of the discharge were taken and an appointment for a mammogram was made for the same day. I thought to myself, They won't find anything and it will all be over. That same evening I was contacted by a doctor in the Kaiser Hayward Clinic, who explained that the mammogram was positive. There was a mass. I was told to schedule a biopsy as soon as possible. My initial reaction was, What if they find something? Something bad?

The biopsy was scheduled for March 1. While I waited for the results I began to wonder how my mother felt as she waited for her results eight years before. Seven days later, I was diagnosed with ductal carcinoma in situ—stage 0 in the breast ducts.

The recommendation for treatment was a total mastectomy with no radiation or chemotherapy. I was referred to a plastic surgeon to further discuss my options. In early April, I consulted with a plastic surgeon who referred me to wonderful surgeon in the Walnut Creek Kaiser Clinic. She told me about a reconstructive procedure called the free TRAM flap, which became my surgical choice. I was referred to another surgeon in the Santa Clara Kaiser Clinic, who took all the time necessary to address my questions and concerns. He then arranged for a team of surgeons and interns to operate on me in mid-May. The surgery on

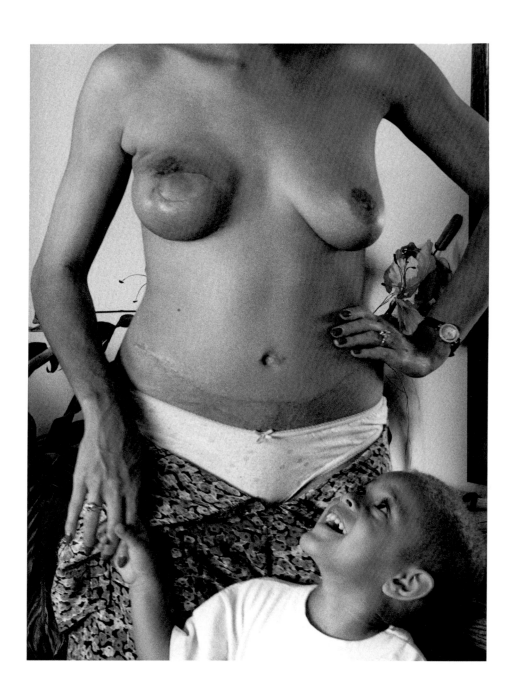

May 16, 1994, was successful. Upon awakening after ten-and-a-half hours of surgery, I wanted to see immediately what my new breast looked like. It was beautiful! Bruised, but beautiful! Many of the surgeons, interns, and nurses would come to my room regularly to see the beautifully sculpted breast. This didn't bother me. In fact, I shared my new breast with friends and family as I praised God for being with me during the whole process.

My two sons, six and three, wanted to see what had happened to Mommy while she was away from home. My six-year-old let me know that he had some understanding of what had happened when he told me that if I had another baby, the baby couldn't have milk from my breast like he did. I smiled and told him he was right.

My husband was afraid at first but with the support of friends and family members he regained the faith that all was going to be fine. Before the surgery he was apprehensive; afterward he was anxious.

Looking back on the whole experience, I feel it happened so fast. During my hospital stay and the six-week period after, I felt privileged to have the opportunity to share my faith with so many people. I feel good about the informed decisions I made along the way. To those who were baffled at how I could laugh and be joyous in the midst of challenge, I say that challenge strengthened my spiritual being.

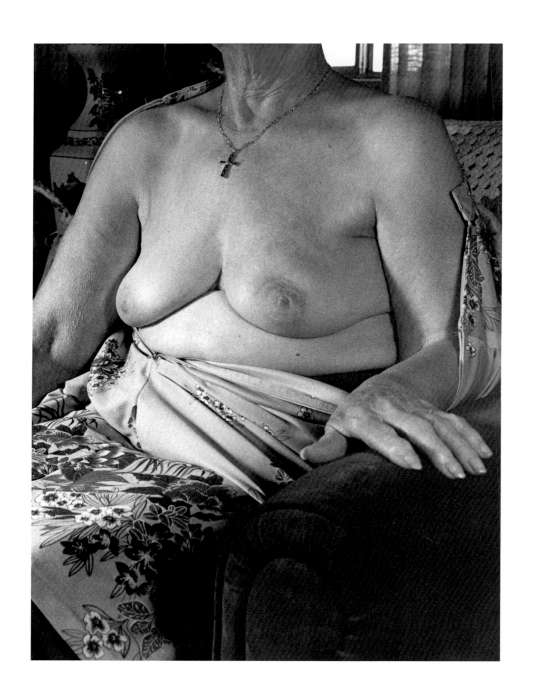

Frances

Breast cancer was the third shock of my life. The first shock was when my husband died fourteen years ago, and the second shock was when my house was robbed.

I had a lumpectomy that became infected and I had to have it drained. I'm on tamoxifen now. The only side effects I have felt from the tamoxifen are hot flashes, which I had for just a short period.

Ruth

I am a breast cancer survivor and this, literally, is my battle scar. I am comfortable with how I look and with my decision to have a mastectomy. While the idea of having a mastectomy may seem terrifying in the abstract, it pales in comparison to a diagnosis of cancer. Once I was diagnosed, survival became my priority. Losing my breast as a means to help save my life was a relatively easy decision to make.

I chose a mastectomy over a lumpectomy primarily because I did not want to subject myself unnecessarily to radiation treatments. I worried about the risk of recurrence in the affected breast as well as that radiation treatments would make it more difficult to read mammograms of that breast. As a relatively young woman, I was also concerned about possible complications arising from scarring of my lung and heart and was troubled that long-term studies were not yet available to identify potential complications that might develop in fifteen or twenty years. Regardless of the reasons for my choice, it is clear to me that my comfort with having had a mastectomy is largely due to the fact that it was my choice, which I was able to make after considering the relative advantages and disadvantages of the various treatment options.

I know from firsthand experience that women are often under pressure to choose against having a mastectomy. I consulted a radiation oncologist who spent more than an hour browbeating me not to "amputate" my breast. He minimized the potential side effects of radiation and portrayed women who chose mastectomy as ignorant and hysterical. I have seen this attitude, in a less extreme form, portrayed numerous times in articles about breast cancer. Lumpectomies are routinely presented as the most medically advanced option, and mastectomies are seen as the

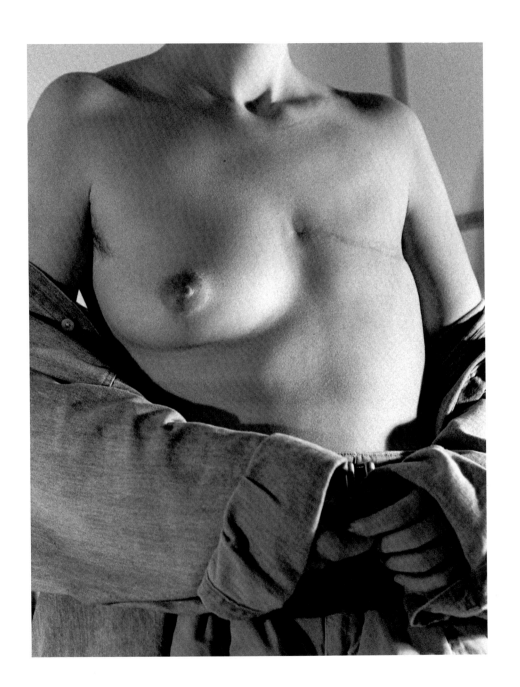

backward choice of frightened women who "blame" their breast for the cancer. Potential side effects of radiation are minimized, if they are discussed at all.

In a society in which we are bombarded with images of large-breasted women in advertisements, movies, and television shows, and little girls grow up playing with impossibly proportioned Barbie dolls, women facing a breast cancer diagnosis are already under tremendous pressure to do anything possible not to lose their breast. There are a variety of reasons why a woman might make an informed choice of a lumpectomy over a mastectomy, but women facing the choice must be given the opportunity to make it with full information and without added pressure. The focus must be on saving the life, not just saving the breast.

Raven Light

FORTY-TWO

At the age of thirty-eight, I assumed my good health was a given. As an avid exhibitionist, I took pride in my appearance, frequently displaying my body publicly in direct fashion statements. Feeling at a sexual peak I looked forward to many more years of desirability and appreciating my body. Then, within three days of learning I had breast cancer, my right breast was amputated. The scar stretches diagonally from beneath my armpit to the middle of my chest. Thirty-three staples held the angry red scar together where once my double D breast had draped down my chest. How could I literally face it? Looking in the mirror became a daily torture. I forced myself to look. A mere five seconds a day loomed like five hours. Touching this alien area was out of the question. My hand behaved like the north end of a magnet approaching the south end. Tears streamed before I could touch my scarred flat chest. Within three weeks of the amputation, I underwent chemo-

therapy that, among other severe side effects, soon stripped me of my beautiful red hair and tore twenty pounds from my already slender body. No eyebrows, no eyelashes, no pubic hair—and no libido. During this time a friend taking Polaroids of my Auschwitzed body commented, "People need to see this," referring to the debacle of my body. "Invisibility will kill us."

The awfulness of these photos haunted me relentlessly for weeks until I decided to turn this personal tragedy into public awareness. Since then I have bared my de-breast in a fierce political stance. Breast cancer has been hidden under heavy layers of shame, guilt, and puffs of cotton stuffed inside empty bras for too many decades. I choose to use my body to put a face on this hideous disease—to stand tall, placing the humanness of breast cancer in everyone's line of sight. My breast and de-breast are seen at parades, on postcards, on the walls of museums, in newspapers and magazines across this country and as far as Zaire. Since 1980 450,000 women have died of breast cancer. As Virginia Soffa stated, "More Americans have died of breast cancer than all the men and women who have died in battle in the Persian Gulf, Vietnam, Korea, and both world wars combined." The rate increases daily.

Breast cancer affects everyBODY, not just middle-class white Americans who can afford insurance payments and annual checkups. The homeless woman with the oxygen tank on the corner may have lost her marginal job because of this largely invisible disease. Conversely, every survivor encompasses more than just a breast cancer causality. We are mothers and lovers, thinkers and teachers, drunkards and dreamers, preachers and prostitutes. We desire and are desirable. I strive to portray myself publicly and politically in a positive light, intending to illustrate to others, and ultimately to myself, that we can still be hot lovers and desirous sexual playmates, breasts or no.

These last four years have been a constant struggle to rebuild a positive relationship with my body. To reintegrate her into my concept of whom I am—that I am not only in my body but that my body is inside of me. Although I have had thousands of people view my body in her entire beauty—scar included—in the privacy of my room, my bedroom mirror still tortures me.

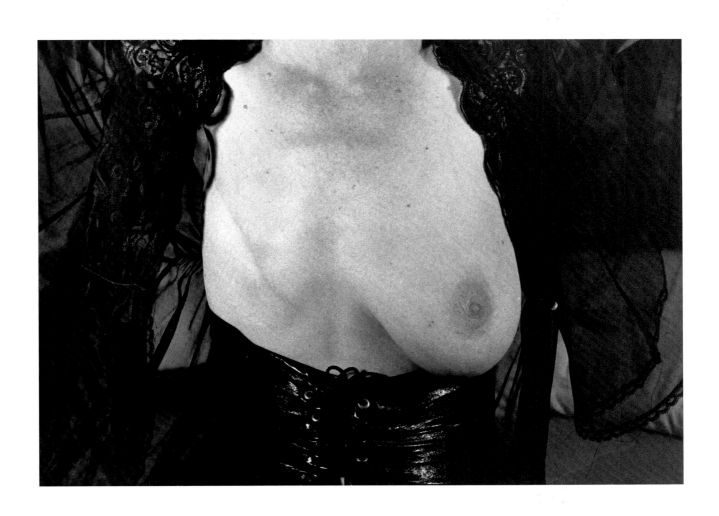

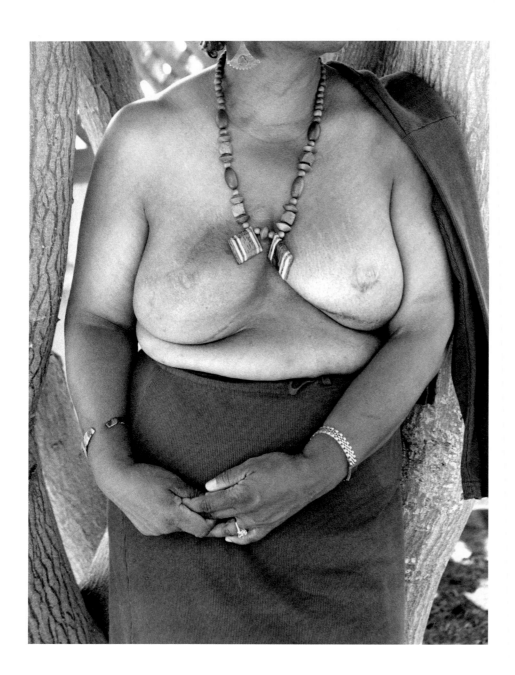

Annette

As I look back on my life, I view it as a series of significant dates and scenarios. I graduated from a San Diego, California, high school in 1957. I was married on July 28, 1956, and gave birth to my first child on September 28, 1957. I gave birth to my second child on May 4, 1959, and to my third child on November 9, 1969.

I went back to school and got a B.A. in social work in 1977 and an M.S. in counselor education in 1979. Currently, I am an Ed.D. candidate in educational leadership.

My husband and I separated in October 1981. Three years later I was diagnosed with breast cancer and underwent a mastectomy on December 10, 1984. I had chemotherapy treatments from March 1985 to December 1985. My husband and I got a divorce on July 28, 1985. I chose to have bilateral reconstructive breast surgery in November 1992.

I have had many spiritual guides along the way: Dr. Katherine Carson, OB-GYN; Dr. David Wile, internist; Dr. Philip Crippen, OB-GYN; Dr. Eugene Rumsey Sr., surgeon; Dr. Martha Simpson, clinical psychologist; Dr. Robert Broulilard, oncologist; Dr. Merton Suzuki, plastic surgeon; Dr. Charlotte Houston, clinical psychologist; the Mercy Hospital staff; and the teachers and staff at Hancock Elementary School.

Many everyday things and family have helped me live with breast cancer: macaroni and cheese, tuna casseroles, and rocky road ice cream; Elsie, my mother; Carol, my sister; Timothy, my son. These things and people helped me through the hair loss, the fatigue, and the weight gain. I learned the value of imagination, relaxation, surrender, forgiveness, and prayer.

I firmly believe my breast cancer experience was a necessary sacred lesson. It has pushed me, nudged me, and propelled me to a greater life. I thank God for the many sacred blessings and the opportunity to grow into greatness. It is with pride that I am a chosen warrior in a life-defining experience.

Merijane

I miss my breast every day.

Being one-breasted is not difficult, but that doesn't mean it's easy. There is one moment in every day—when I remove my pajamas to step into the bathtub in the morning or when I pull my shirt over my head to undress for the night—when I am still shocked to see my asymmetrical chest.

The mastectomy was my fourth surgery: two excisional biopsies, one lumpectomy, eight weeks of radiation, and finally, two-and-a-half years later, the amputation. I fought hard to keep my breast and gave it up only when it seemed absolutely necessary. There's no way of knowing if it was—the cancer metastasized to my spine less than twelve months later.

This photograph was taken six weeks after the mastectomy. Within two years, the thin red line faded to white. The skin is supple after daily self-massage; the left side of my chest is a series of soft and hard ripples. I'm no longer surprised at how loud my heartbeat sounds without the soft cushion of my breast to muffle it. I often wear jewelry where my breast used to be; I do not wear a prosthesis. I go naked to the women's baths and wonder what the bathers think and feel when they see me. Am I their worst fear? Do they silently applaud me for my courage or resent me for making them look at something they would rather not confront?

I feel strongly that we *must* be seen. Breast cancer, and the effects of treatment, have been hidden long enough. The wounds are quickly covered with "breast forms" or "reconstruction," as if they are a secret we

59

must keep from each other and the world, as if the solution is merely cosmetic. An advertisement I have seen too often in magazines shows a diverse group of women with breast cancer who have, according to the advertiser, boosted their self-esteem by learning to hide their cancer with cosmetics, wigs, and creative ways of wearing scarves. We may laugh at the sheer absurdity of this message, but it is as insidious as breast cancer itself.

There is still no cure for breast cancer. All the technology intended to make us "beautiful" after we have been cut, radiated, and filled with toxic chemicals does not alter that fact. Until the *real* causes of this disease—the human-made, environmental causes—are addressed with commitment and sincerity, the word *prevention* holds no meaning.

I don't know if I will die from breast cancer, but I do know that, day to day, I am *living* with it.

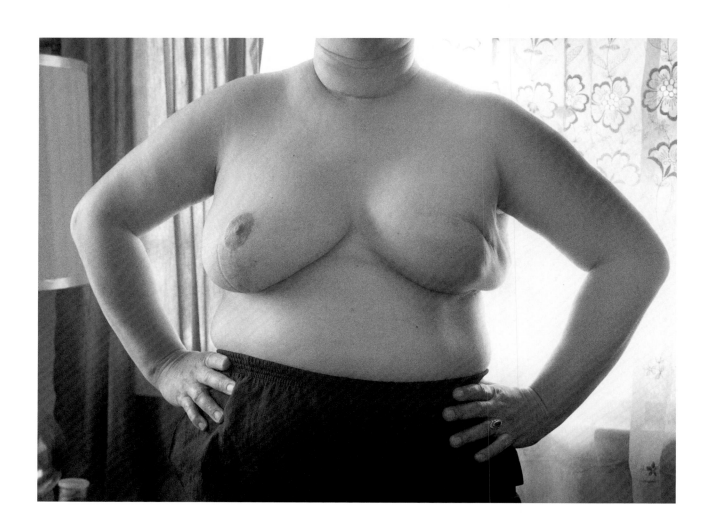

Marleen

FORTY-EIGHT

The fight is not only cancer. The fight is not only fate.
They need to be heard and seen. The time is already late.
She is the silent soldier—the invisible amputee.
She is every woman; she is you, she is me.

—Marleen M. Quint,
"Silent Soldier—Invisible Amputee"

I remember feeling like a broken doll during all five operations and the eighteen months it took to "reconstruct" me. I was no longer a person, but more like a Raggedy Ann doll blown apart in a battle that was taking place somewhere in the Twilight Zone.

It all began with a bleeding milk duct in my left breast. I was told I had only a 3 percent chance of having breast cancer. I ended up with a lumpectomy, then a modified radical mastectomy with seventeen lymph nodes removed, then multiple reconstruction surgeries, including a breast reduction on the right side to match the reconstructed breast. I now have more surface scars on my healthy breast than on the cancer-affected breast.

I've heard it said that many women believe they are ultimately better people for having had breast cancer. I am not one of these women. I am a minority female

(Portuguese Pacific Islander) who has survived many hardships and ill health. I did not need a life-threatening disease, which was treated with procedures that are also life threatening, to help me approach life with more grace and appreciation.

It would be interesting to poll men who are living with advanced prostate cancer. I'd wager you'd be hard pressed to find one who believed he was a better man for having survived such an intimate disease through the use of dangerous and impotent-rendering treatments.

We cannot achieve true grace until we fully acknowledge those things that threaten to oppress and destroy us. Breast cancer is treated with aggression and destruction rather than healing through nurturing. Remember that surgery attacks with a blade, chemotherapy was originally a World War II poison called mustard gas, and radiation is a known carcinogen that burns and destroys tissue. We use the same approach and weapons for medicine as we do for war. These photos are a testimony to the assault we call breast cancer treatment.

I would be a much better woman knowing that we've found a cause, prevention, and a real cure for breast cancer. On that day I can live with a greater sense of self-worth and accept my eventual mortality with grace. On that day I can die knowing I was leaving a more promising legacy to my daughter and the generations to come.

Maxine

One night in December 1961 my husband said to me, "You have a lump in your breast." I was only thirty-five years old and breast cancer didn't enter my mind. It didn't hurt and I felt foolish going to the doctor. My husband insisted that I go. When I went in January 1962 I asked the surgeon what percentage of these lumps are cancer and he answered, "About 10 percent." That is all I heard. Of course I didn't have cancer, I thought. While I was on the operating table a biopsy was done. The results of the biopsy sent the doctor out to tell my husband that it was cancer and they would do a radical mastectomy.

When I woke up in the recovery room the doctor came in and told me, "We did the big operation." My first fear was how my husband would feel about it. No one explained what would happen after the surgery. I thought something must be really wrong. I felt like my arm was broken and that I had a tight band across my chest. This pain came from the removal of part of the pectoral muscle. The third day after surgery the doctor came in and said I would need radiation followed by removal of the ovaries. That was my worst day. I broke down and cried, wondering if I would live long enough to raise my three sons, ages two-and-a-half, eight, and eleven. I kept my feelings to myself when around my family, but it was hard. I felt I had to keep a stiff upper lip. Now I know better.

I went home ten days later and started X-ray treatments. Members of the PTA and my church took turns driving me, as my husband had just started a new job and was traveling a lot. The x-ray treatments caused severe burns that kept forming blisters for some time after the treatments had ended. Around this time my second son had joined Cub Scouts and I wanted to go to the Blue and Gold Dinner so badly but just didn't have the energy. I felt I had let him down.

65

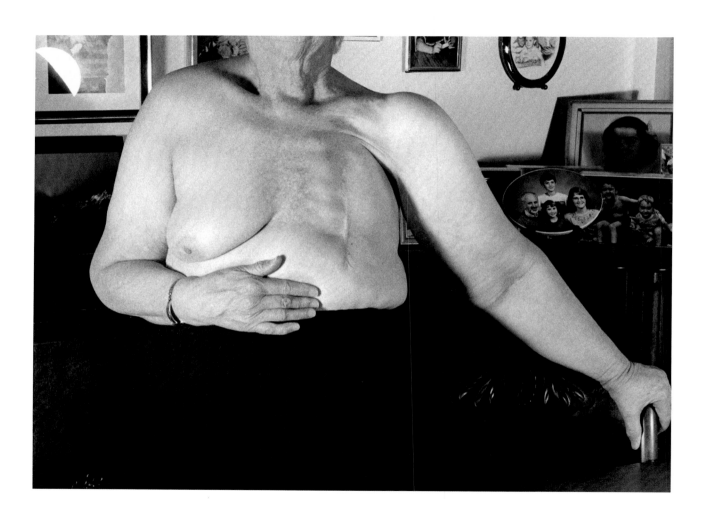

The day after Easter my ovaries were removed, as the cancer was a hormone-related type. That was the worst of the whole experience—going immediately into menopause with drenching hot flashes, fatigue, and headaches. When I mentioned it to the doctor he said, "That is just menopause." Nobody told me what to expect after breast cancer or menopause. I went to the library and read everything I could about the subject. I have learned more working as a Reach to Recovery volunteer for the past sixteen years than I did then. I didn't get information on osteoporosis from the doctor until I asked him about it fifteen years ago.

I need larger sleeves due to lymphedema and high necks in clothes to cover the hole under my collarbone. Jackets look longer on the left side because that shoulder is sunken in. I asked for my pathology report five years ago and found out that I had an infiltrating ductal carcinoma with lymph node metastases. My husband told me then that after my surgery the doctor told him the cancer would probably go to my lungs. He kept that to himself for thirty-three years. What a burden for him! After over thirty-four years I am going strong and have had no recurrence.

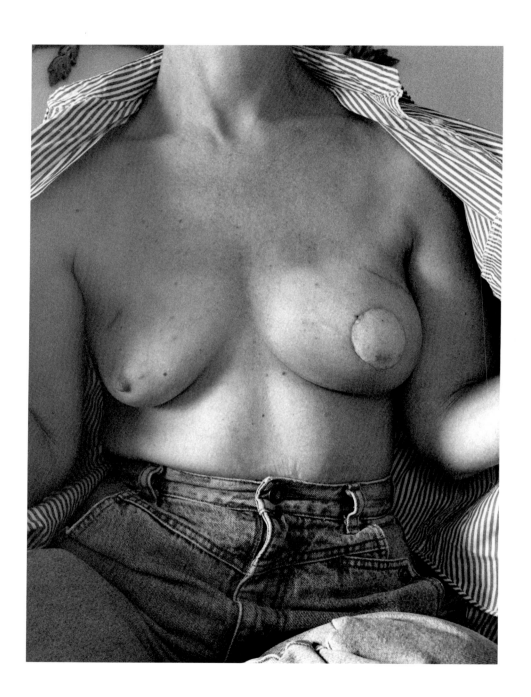

Paula

FORTY-NINE

My cancer was discovered during a routine yearly mammogram. I could not believe I had cancer since I was so good about monthly self-exams and yearly mammograms. I asked myself, Why me? and, What did I do wrong?

I have since learned, however, that because of my careful monitoring, my cancer was found at the earliest possible stage.

After my diagnosis, I was told I had time to research my options, which I did. I chose to have a mastectomy with immediate reconstruction. I am so pleased with my choice because I never saw my body without a breast. I awoke from my surgery with a breast and because of this I have never felt like a cancer patient.

It has been four-and-a-half weeks since my cancer surgery. I feel like my old self again, and I attribute this to my reconstruction.

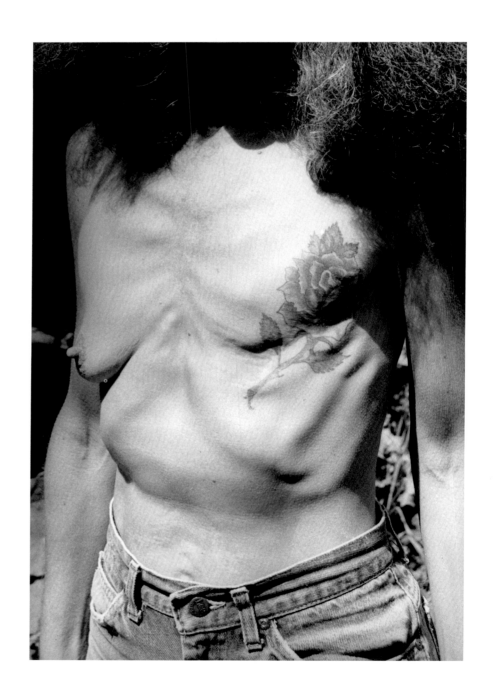

Andrée

They said, "Don't worry about it." I didn't. Then the tiny lump under my skin—benign for twelve years, through four doctors and four mammograms—transformed into cancer. "It can't happen," said the doctors. It happened. So a mastectomy, and so chemotherapy: an adventure in the life-saving miseries of medicine.

Contemporary sages tell us that men value their bodies' action parts, women their pretty parts. Those sages don't know me. I dance in the woods, play flute on the sea's cliffs, write words with my left hand: these I prize. My left breast did none of these things, but it was a conduit for sensual pleasure. My right breast had taken over its duties, light as they are since chemotherapy had its way with my sexuality. My left breast has transformed itself into a red rose—sacred—which grows in my dreams.

My mind embraces this rose and everything that came before.

My beloved loves breasts but he loves life more, perhaps especially my life. He didn't want me to go, so he said good-bye to my breast with certain equanimity. He suggested getting the tattoo. The rose suggested itself. It whispered, "It's the genocide, not the tits, darling. Let's show them the invisible epidemic, the woman-killer."

While breast cancer, the invisible killer, elicits fear and loathing, this rose elicits uneasy smiles. The crowd applauds; I pick up my flute and seduce the sea. Then I create the world anew with my pen, but the rose intrudes even there with its beautiful warning. It asks, "What but death is the end of the world?"

A flashback: Coming home from the hospital with my brand new mastectomy, we stop at an intersection to let a beautiful young woman cross the street. She has two perfect breasts under her T-shirt and she breaks my heart. The left leg of her designer jeans is pinned up against her body: the entire leg has been amputated, apparently recently. She's new at her crutches; she's through dancing. As she crosses the street awkwardly, her friend says something and she laughs.

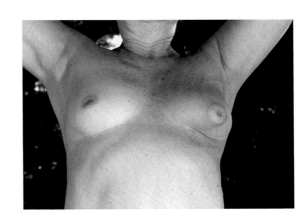

BREAST RECONSTRUCTION

Loren Eskenazi, M.D., F.A.C.S.

Who can best describe the loss of a breast? Only those women who have experienced it. These women know that the breast is more than just an organ, a part of the body that provides sustenance to a newborn. It is also a symbol representing motherhood, nurturing femininity, fertility, and sexuality.

Breast cancer is a transformative experience. It is traumatic, unpleasant, and unwanted. We would all rather do without it. However, like a tribal initiation or a rite of passage, it is a doorway through which one passes into a new life.

Even though I am a plastic surgeon, I do not focus solely on the medical aspects of breast cancer as I prepare for surgery. I am aware that my patient lies upon an operating table (similar to an altar) and undergoes anesthesia (a trancelike state). For me cancer is an awe-inspiring process that does not end in the recovery room. The healing and transformation go on for years—perhaps a lifetime—and affect the woman, her family and friends, and the health care professionals involved in her case. Unfortunately, healing is not always synonymous with a cure, but I have been impressed that regardless of the outcome, healing does occur on physical, spiritual, and social levels.

Despite its focus, this book is about much more than breast cancer. It is about renewal, resilience, and regeneration. It is also about reality—not the way we want life to be, but the way it is. The photographs in this book may not always be pretty to look at, but the women and their stories are beautiful nonetheless. Although these women are not my patients, like mine they represent women of all ages, socioeconomic groups, and walks of life.

Like my patients, these women have faced surgery and the prospect of losing a breast. Fortunately, surgical treatment options today range from lumpectomy to mastectomy, and reconstructive choices are numerous. Before undergoing surgery, every woman needs to have adequate information about immediate reconstruction versus a delayed procedure, reconstruction using her own tissue, and implants so that she can pick the treatment that is right for her.

Though women may elect to have reconstruction after a lumpectomy, women choose reconstruction most commonly following a mastectomy. Once a woman has decided upon a mastectomy with her general surgeon, she can consider immediate reconstruction, which is performed at the same time as her mastectomy. Patients with extremely large tumors or tumors very close to the chest wall may not be candidates for immediate reconstruction, but virtually everyone else, regardless of breast size, body weight, or age, is. Since Congress passed a law in 1999 requiring insurance companies to cover breast reconstruction, financial circumstances will be a decisive

factor for fewer women when they choose between treatment options.

Immediate reconstruction offers numerous advantages over a delayed procedure. First, a woman will wake up from surgery with two breasts. Although the reconstructed breast will not have a nipple on it and may not be exactly the size of the other one initially, its presence in the immediate post-operative period can speed overall recovery and improve psychological well-being.

Second, patients who choose immediate reconstruction virtually always have less scarring than those who choose delayed reconstruction. It is even possible for the reconstruction to be completed with no visible scars on the breast. Scarring is virtually eliminated with a skin-sparing mastectomy, in which the nipple and breast tissue are removed and the rest of the breast skin is filled with abdominal fatty tissue, back tissue, or a breast implant. Figures 1–4 show the differences between immediate and delayed reconstruction. The patient in these photos had a mastec-

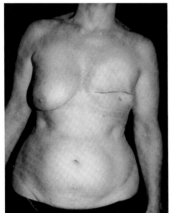

Figure 1

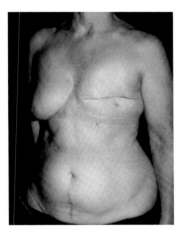

Figure 2

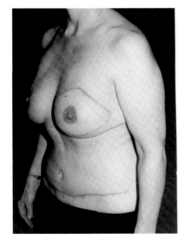

Figure 3

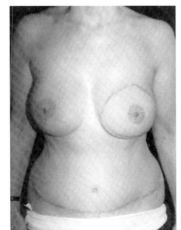

Figure 4

tomy on the left side, then developed a precancerous lesion in her right breast several years later. Both breasts were reconstructed at the same time. Her right breast tissue was removed and the skin was filled with abdominal fat. Her left breast reconstruction required skin from her abdomen since the breast skin was discarded during the earlier mastectomy. As is evident from figures 3 and 4, there are no visible scars on her right breast (the immediate reconstruction), but there are large scars on her left breast (the delayed reconstruction).

The advantages of using tissue from the abdomen during reconstruction, called a TRAM flap (transverse rectus myocutaneous flap), include the avoidance of long-term maintenance and a more natural feel and appearance to the breast. A breast made out of abdominal tissue is warm and soft, moves like a normal breast, and gains or loses weight as the patient gains or loses it. Another advantage is that removal of the abdominal tissue in effect gives the patient a tummy tuck, which flattens the lower abdomen. To most women the tummy tuck is a welcome by-product of the TRAM flap operation.

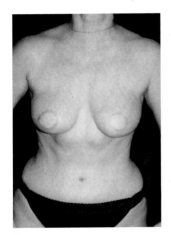

Figure 5

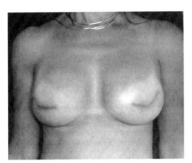

Figure 6

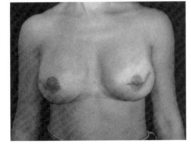

Figure 7

Figure 5 shows a woman just a few weeks after having both her breasts reconstructed using a TRAM flap. The scars where the nipples were removed are evident now and the small circles of abdominal skin have not yet been tattooed. Once the nipples are reconstructed, however, the scars will be invisible. The woman in figure 6, in contrast, had bilateral implant reconstructions a few weeks before this photograph was taken. Although the scars can vary in size and location following these procedures, most women will have a straight scar. Small scars will remain on either side of the reconstructed nipples (see figure 7).

The disadvantages of a TRAM flap include a longer surgery (three to six hours) than is necessary for insertion of an implant, a longer recovery, and postoperative pain in the abdomen. The hospital stay is three to five days and the recovery period is six to twelve weeks, depending on the patient. Although it is a relatively rare complication, the abdomen may also require repair at a later date. This complication may be dependent on the technique the plastic surgeon used to close the area where the abdominal tissue was removed.

For women with little abdominal fat, options for reconstruction include flaps from other parts of the body. For very small breasted women, using the back muscle alone (called a latissimus flap) might suffice, but more often an implant must be placed beneath the back flap so that the reconstructed breast matches the other one. If skin from the buttock is used a small artery and vein from the buttock must be transferred with the tissue and sewn to an artery and vein in the armpit area (this is called a microsurgical or free flap). The operation is a demanding one and usually leaves a significant scar or indentation in the buttock area. In my opinion, this should be reserved as a last resort because it is a long operation and because a breast made from the buttock is often less natural in appearance than one constructed from abdominal tissue. It is also possible to use tissue from the outer thigh (called a Rubens flap), but this is rarely done.

Women who choose implants rather than reconstruction using their own tissue recover from the surgery faster and do not have scarring on other parts of their bodies where tissue has been taken. A mastectomy and insertion of an implant takes about three hours, and the hospital stay is one or two nights. Usually no blood transfusion is required. However, implants will virtually always need some later maintenance surgery due to hardening (encapsulation) or leakage. This surgery may be necessary within a few years or after a period of ten or more years and may have to be done more than once. A breast with an implant may look quite natural, depending on the skill of the plastic surgeon, but it will never feel as natural as a breast reconstructed from the patient's tissue.

Implants can be filled with silicone, saline, or a combination of both and come in fixed sizes or adjustable versions. Although some women worry about the safety of silicone implants, the FDA has never withdrawn them from the market for use in women diagnosed with cancer. Even during the height of the silicone controversy the FDA maintained that the benefits of these implants outweighed the potential risks. Silicone's primary advantage over saline is that it feels and looks more natural. This consistency is important because the skin and muscle over the implant is quite thin and there is no breast tissue or fat to cover it.

If an immediate reconstruction is performed using a skin-sparing mastectomy, a post-operatively adjustable implant (filled with either all saline or a saline-silicone mixture) is often used. This type of implant allows the surgeon to inject it with additional saline after the surgery to fine-tune the breast's size and symmetry. When this process is completed (usually after six to eight weeks), the injection port, a small plastic piece the size of a nickel, is removed and the nipple is reconstructed. This second operation most often requires only local anesthesia and is done on an outpatient basis. If the patient is not satisfied with the look and feel of the adjustable implant, it can be exchanged for one of a different size or for a silicone implant at this point. Surgery to change an implant is almost always shorter and less painful than the first operation since the first one requires the release of the pectoralis chest muscle from its surrounding structures so that the implant can be placed beneath it.

Instead of inserting a silicone or saline implant during the first surgery, some surgeons prefer to use an expander, which is an implant designed to temporarily stretch the skin on the chest. Although this makes a breast that is too big initially, the expander is easily removed and replaced with an implant of the appropriate size. Completion of this type of reconstruction usually means three to four operations, while performing a skin-sparing mastectomy and inserting a post-operatively adjustable implant takes only two. Delayed reconstructions, which are performed months or years after a mastectomy, almost always require that the skin be stretched with an expander.

Another important consideration when making decisions about treatment is that radiation therapy limits reconstructive options. Before a patient agrees to undergo radiation therapy she should be aware that reconstruction with an implant is usually not possible afterward. When implants are used after radiation women are much more likely to experience complications. Most often women are advised to use their own tissue to reconstruct a breast after this therapy. For some women this is simply not an option, but it should be employed whenever possible.

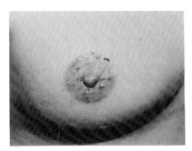

Figure 8

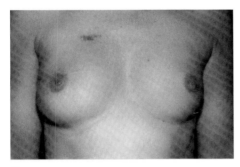

Figure 9

Most reconstructed nipples are formed from tissue already present on the breast mound that is then tattooed to match the nipple and areola color of the opposite breast. For women with relatively large nipples, it is also possible to take a small graft from the normal breast. In my experience, a nipple graft with tattoo for the areola gives the most natural result and virtually never leaves a detectable scar or disturbs sensation in the normal breast. Other options include a skin graft from the groin or labia area (most often called a Skate flap), which may need to be tattooed at a later date. Not all surgeons do their own tattooing at the time of the nipple reconstruction, but instead refer their patients to a nurse or esthetician skilled in this cosmetic procedure. Figure 8 shows a reconstructed nipple made from breast skin that was later tattooed. The right nipple in figure 9 is made from a nipple graft and the areola has been tattooed.

Women with breast cancer should keep in mind that each woman is unique and the appropriate reconstructive technique depends on lifestyle, body type, and personal circumstances at the time of diagnosis.

So many options can make the decision confusing and there is often no one "right" answer. The best you can do as a patient is to become educated about the risks and benefits of each procedure and make the decision that instinctively feels right. Trusting your intuition is essential, but it does not take the place of good information and competent physicians. Places to start looking for help are the organizations, Web sites, and publications listed in the Resources section of this book; local support groups; and the advice of friends, family, and physicians. A personal recommendation is always the best way to choose a physician, and almost everyone knows someone whose life has been touched by breast cancer. Most of all, do not be afraid to ask questions and explore your options.

Figures courtesy of Loren Eskenazi

LYMPHEDEMA

Saskia R. J. Thiadens, R. N.

It is difficult enough to lose a breast, but the possibility of also living with a chronically swollen arm for the rest of their lives is more than many women can accept. Fortunately, more effective treatments and resources are becoming available to help women live with the physical, psychological, and social consequences of this condition.

Today there are over 2 million breast cancer survivors in the United States. It is estimated that over 20 percent have secondary lymphedema (swelling in the arm), which can develop after axillary lymph node surgery, often if it is combined with radiation. Lymphedema has been defined as an abnormal collection of tissue protein in the body due to an interruption or obstruction of the lymphatic vessels by a tumor or inflammation. The degree of swelling can be mild to severe and can occur immediately in the post-treatment period or months or even years later. Untreated, the affected limb can become very large and heavy, and the skin will lose its elasticity. In addition, upper-extremity lymphedema predisposes women to the development of often serious acute and chronic infections. Although lymphedema is incurable, it can be treated.

The search for the most effective therapy for lymphedema is ongoing. During the 1990s, for instance, many medical professionals adopted Complete Decongestive Therapy (CDT), a European modality considered the most helpful. CDT consists of manual lymphatic drainage, bandaging, remedial exercise, skin care, good nutrition, and education in home self-care techniques so that the patient can be independent. Once the limb has been decongested, the patient should wear a compression sleeve during the day to keep the swelling from returning. Most important is for the patient to be educated about what to do—and not do—before, during, and after breast cancer surgery. She should avoid having her blood pressure measured using the affected arm; she should offer her other arm for injections and blood tests; she should avoid heavy lifting; she should wear gloves in the garden and while working in the kitchen to prevent cuts that might lead to infection; and she should stay alert to symptoms that might indicate early lymphedema, such as a watch or ring that is too tight. Many women wear a lymphedema alert bracelet to make the public and health care professionals aware that there should be no needle sticks or blood pressure measurements in the affected arm.

Lymphedema clinics with certified therapists are becoming more common, and complex decongestive therapies are becoming more readily available. Breast cancer patients should consult with their physicians and local breast cancer support groups about sources of information and the latest options for treatment of lymphedema.

Organizations

American Cancer Society. 800-227-2345. Brochures and other material; referrals to local groups.

American Indian Women's Health Demonstration Project. 415-865-0964. Health and wellness education program for Native American women.

Breast Cancer Action. 415-243-9301 or 877-2STOPBC (toll free). Education and advocacy organization founded and led by women living with breast cancer; bimonthly newsletter, public forums.

The Breast Cancer Fund. 415-543-2979. Raises funding for cutting-edge research, patient support, education, and advocacy efforts.

Breast Cancer Resource Committee. 202-463-8040.

The Mautner Project for Lesbians with Cancer. 202-332-5536. Education, information, and advocacy on special concerns of lesbians with cancer and their families.

National Alliance of Breast Cancer Organizations. 888-80-NABCO. Information about breast cancer and referrals for women with breast cancer.

National Asian Women's Health Organization. 415-989-9747.

National Cancer Institute's Cancer Information Service. 800-4-CANCER. Advice on diagnoses, treatment options, and availability of clinical trials.

National Latina Health Organization. 510-534-1362.

National Lymphedema Network. 800-541-3259. Information and treatment about prevention and treatment of lymphedema, the most common long-term complication of breast cancer. Guidelines and referrals for medical treatment, physical therapy, and support.

Sisters Network. 713-781-0255. Support, education, and advocacy for African American women with breast cancer; outreach, training, and research; assistance in starting new groups.

Susan G. Koman Breast Cancer Foundation. 800-I'M AWARE. Research, information, and awareness about breast cancer; sponsor of Race for the Cure in major cities.

Women's Cancer Resource Center. 510-548-9272. TTY line for the deaf. Information, referral, support, and advocacy to meet the needs of all women with cancer, particularly the poor, the elderly, women of color, and lesbians.

Y-ME National Breast Cancer Organization. 800-221-2141 (day) or 312-986-8228 (24 hrs.). Information and peer support for women with breast cancer.

Young Survival Coalition. 212-577-6259.

Books

Steve Austin and Cathy Hitchcock, *Breast Cancer: What You Should Know (But May Not Be Told) about Prevention, Diagnosis, and Treatment* (Rocklin, Calif.: Prima, 1994).

Nancy Bruning, *Coping with Chemotherapy* (Garden City, N.Y.: Dial Press, 1985).

Michael Lerner, *Choices in Healing: Integrating the Best of Conventional and Complementary Approaches to Cancer* (Cambridge, Mass.: MIT Press, 1994).

John Link, M.D., *The Breast Cancer Survival Manual: A Step-by-Step Guide for the Woman with Newly Diagnosed Breast Cancer* (New York: Henry Holt, 1998).

Susan M. Love with Karen Lindsay, *Dr. Susan Love's Breast Book,* 2d ed. (Reading, Mass.: Addison-Wesley, 1995).

Musa Mayer, *Holding Tight, Letting Go: Living with Metastatic Breast Cancer* (Sebastopol, Calif.: O'Reilly, 1997).

Web Sites

American Cancer Society
   http://www.cancer.org

Breast Cancer Action
   http://www.bcaction.org

The Breast Cancer Fund
   http://www.breastcancerfund.org

Community Breast Health Project
   http://www-med.stanford.edu/CBHP

The Mautner Project for Lesbians with Cancer
   http://www.mautnerproject.org

National Alliance of Breast Cancer Organizations
   http://www.nabco.org

National Cancer Institute's Cancer Information
   Service
   http://cis.nci.nih.gov/contact/contact.html

National Lymphedema Network
   http://www.lymphnet.org

Susan G. Koman Breast Cancer Foundation
   http://www.koman.org

University of Pennsylvania Cancer Center
   http://www.oncolink.upenn.edu

Y-ME National Breast Cancer Organization
   http://www.y-me.org

Young Survival Coalition
   http://www.youngsurvival.org

AMELIA DAVIS is a professional photographer based in San Francisco. Her work, including that on breast cancer survivors, has been featured in magazines, textbooks, and a number of solo and group exhibitions.

NANCY SNYDERMAN, M.D., is a medical correspondent for ABC News and can be seen on "Good Morning America" and "20/20." She also writes a monthly column for *Good Housekeeping* and is a medical contributor to *Health*.

LOREN ESKENAZI, M.D. F.A.C.S., is a plastic and reconstructive surgeon in practice in San Francisco and is a member of the clinical faculty at Stanford University. She has appeared frequently on local and national television and radio and has authored many scientific publications on breast reconstruction as well as articles for magazines including the *Economist, Allure, Vogue,* and *Cosmopolitan.*

SASKIA R. J. THIADENS, R.N., is a registered nurse and the executive director of the National Lymphedema Network, which she founded in 1988. She is also the founder of the Aurora Lymphedema Clinic.

Typeset in 11/16 Perpetua
with Carpenter display
Designed by Copenhaver Cumpston
Composed at the University of Illinois Press
Printed in duotone on 80# Luna Matte
by Friesens Corporation

University of Illinois Press
1325 South Oak Street
Champaign, IL 61820-6903
WWW.PRESS.UILLINOIS.EDU